The
REFLECTING
Pool

The REFLECTING Pool

Maleea Acker

PEDLAR PRESS | Toronto

For Carmel and Woody at Maltby, with love,
Maleea
Spring 2023

COPYRIGHT © 2009 Maleea Acker

ALL RIGHTS RESERVED. No part of this book may be reproduced or transmitted in any form or by any means whatsoever without written permission from the publisher, except by a reviewer, who may quote brief passages in a review. For information, write Pedlar Press at PO Box 26, Station P, Toronto Ontario M5S 2S6 Canada.

ACKNOWLEDGEMENTS
The publisher wishes to thank the Canada Council for the Arts and the Ontario Arts Council for their generous support of our publishing program.

LIBRARY AND ARCHIVES CANADA
CATALOGUING IN PUBLICATION

Acker, Maleea, 1975-
   The reflecting pool / Maleea Acker.

Poems.

ISBN 978-1-897141-29-8

   I. Title.

PS8601.C535R44 2009   C811'.6   C2009-903392-5

DESIGN Zab Design & Typography, Toronto
TYPEFACE Montrachet, by Fountain Type Foundry

Printed in Canada

Contents

AMONG FORESTS AND FIELDS 13

one

TRADUCCIÓN 17

CALLES DE MÉRIDA A LAS TRES DE LA MAÑANA 18

A LAS TRES DE LA MAÑANA 19

HAPPENSTANCE 20

SMALL FAILURES 21

HISTORY 24

ALPUJARRA 25

two

KALEIDOSCOPE 31

REGARD 32

IF THERE IS SOMETHING 33

SUMMER NIGHT 34

GRADUATES: ST. PETER'S 35

SPRING MIGRATION, IN THE FIELD 36

NIGHT WALK 37

WEB 38

SKY AND THE VARIED THRUSH 39

MEASURE 40

WINTER: ARIA DA CAPO 42

LIES IN THE FIELD LIKE THE SKY 44

three

THEORY 53

STARS: CHILDHOOD 54

STATION 55

LETTER TO LUKE, WHO IS HERE WITH ME IN BUBIÓN 57

RETURN OF THE NUTHATCHES 59

CONSIDERING MY FATHER 61

THIS PERFORMANCE OF ROWING THROUGH THE DARK AND STARS 62

AS WATER IS TO INLANDS 64

WHEN ALL IS SAID OR DONE 66

THE REFLECTING POOL 68

four

LATE AUGUST: YIELDING 73

RIVER, BUT NO EDGE 74

THE REFLECTING POOL,
MOUNT HELMCKEN: AFTERWORD 75

Summer Variations

    WORK 79

    TRILL 81

    STILLNESS 83

    SILENCE 85

    RUMMAGE 86

NOTES & ACKNOWLEDGEMENTS 89

But today my gaze has left me.
My blindness has gone away.
The dark bat has left my face and is scissoring around
   in summer's bright space.

   —Tomas Tranströmer

At last the fidelity of things opens our eyes

   —Zbigniew Herbert

AMONG FORESTS AND FIELDS

I look and look to the page, then turn, see
myself reflected in the window of the studio.

Dusk and the dark firs waving at me.
Night and the dark firs waving at me.

All kinds of pictures and poems on the walls.
Nest of necessity, curling around the room.

To search and search for this beauty,
then discover the girl alone. O firs, O black night,

the tug of the wire attached to the skull,
it hauls light up ever higher, emanates

heat from its core; firs, black night and
reflecting pool of window, forgive me.

One

TRADUCCIÓN

Map lines: their cross hatchings, intersections, throughways,
dead ends—they imply space and time

in one instant. Ours was the happening in between,
a diffusion of streets into history, an environment

defined by you, unrolling, alleys not drawn but born.
Light switches flipped in dark rooms. In the fissure

of a wall, a garden—water fell from a leaking drainpipe
to the broken concrete below. Ferns, moss, a bundle

of roots inched themselves into the built,
through a lens. The lights of occasional cars

trailed through air as long-exposure photographs.
Behind street lamp, vacant building—

each story an intangible interior, we are
more than the sum of what we can record.

CALLES DE MÉRIDA A LAS TRES DE LA MAÑANA

This is a time of grace: to remember the weaving lights
of sepia cars during our hours of night translation.

The yellow street lamps' glimmer falls, purifies each wandering dog,
every drunk with arms around basket or love,

and settles between us like an animal curling for rest;
circle, circle, drop into somewhere spirit knows

to be full. A fine dust on all; construction of the new city,
splinters, stones and machinery of the dark, amassing

every hour. It rebuilds itself to glow like the sun,
roomy, two names for each one. A raven web

of telephone wire connects us. Every word
increases until it shines like copper, attentive—

it permeates the surface of all things until they flame.
We reach eager for what centre we contain.

A LAS TRES DE LA MAÑANA

By yielding to the language, we understand the other.
At three in the morning the city cools to accept us;

we stumble through like dogs, hunch, touch one another
wherever we can. Clarity is a chapel of these stars,

low above amber buildings, rusting iron doors.
Articulation, transmutation of phrase, the scrape

of boot on gravel. I wake from where I have folded
on my own arm, the listening a whole, corporeal longing.

These are bicycle hours, the streets empty,
a pedal clutched in the quiet; each wheel languid,

backward, inviting meaning in
as a train makes a landscape go by.

Another set of words drives its way home,
meshes: the mind surrenders.

Not of the light, we let ourselves be placated,
to uphold the names, to keep the steps aloft.

HAPPENSTANCE

A month before, first snow in my north. A skin of ice
grew over the lake, delicate; green geese skimmed through.

Geometry of winter, black twig-strokes, nothingness
settling into a long-night dream of abundance.

Meanwhile, the first migrant thrushes whistled at your window.
Their song an awkward gesture, mechanical wings

over water and mountain clicking the land into relation.
The hurricane over Mérida evaporated. Ruined roads

sloshed into the mangrove, bird shadows fell in patterns
from uprooted trees. Dusk tilted into a calm sea,

its memory of wind a net not mended. There will be no wall
of water, no fishes in the air—only our shadows,

auratic, lofted over water, at ease, yielding to air.

SMALL FAILURES

From these fragmented conversations where you are absent
    I offer, this morning, the Yucatán:
we are wrapped inside the bus's shell,
hurtling through the heat of day.
      Pulse of broken centre line,
bright reflection of window sears the grasses and trash,
words you may understand: *Mérida, Santa Clara,
Vallidolíd*, where we go into the Virgin of Candelaría's home.
The altar's perpetual dusk—
small flames we gravitate toward,
our approach
          shoulder with miracle.
It unfurls into the arches of each ponderous dome,
a space of silence beyond
cobwebs, birds. A church at noon, spectacular
         understatement of desire.

Thirty kilometres north of Progreso last month,
the hurricane found its true mark
              plundered the coastline
from San Crisanto to Uaymitún, rearranging roads, swept
cars through cornfields,
a final migration of birds
        pinned to the scrub bush roots of mangrove.

Near river and altered coastline, we stop briefly: a hotel
with ground windows blown out by the sea, tide line sketching
each bed, patio glass strewn over the sand.

The same force that created us, turning
and turning again, builds beyond our failures, until
someone presses the light switch
in an abandoned room a month later, and the whole town relaxes,
            with snap and pulse,
                        into darkness.
Take my hand. The concrete where it has
            fallen into the sea
is not steady, and we may need
to help one another.

Maybe what we fear is
            not force but a quiet leaving,
a far summer storm at night, lightning visible,
the air calm, the flash
            inconsequential.
We fall through the barrier,
            someone's beginning, their skin
permeable, receiving another.

The bus stops. We go in
to a concrete shelter to shed clothes.
Grasses line the water's edge;
arc of birdsong, calls we have not heard,

fish rising to the surface
                then falling to darkness—
I go down to meet them.

Indivisible, our story
from happenstance; having
never entered church or lake together, having
history only through words,
        which weave themselves,
                which *begin*.
On the far side of the lake
water is rooted and green; there is no cleaving

of edge from edge—the forest a pool of green, the lake
home to trees. We return to Mérida
as dusk falls and a trick of the light creates
a tableau of house, street, child, dog:
a photograph
        I offer you;
indistinguishable in the twilight.

HISTORY

The pin enters to carve the hole
In the wood of a window frame,

Ballast for roses, letter, card.
Wood moves aside for metal and holds,

Waits. One hundred years go by.
Wood dries, shambles against itself,

Opens—cave, nest, history, gate—
Into itself, apparent, lets go the art.

It starts so small, then gives way.
Cup and thrust, darkness into the world.

ALPUJARRA

The girl who sings in the evenings
warms up her voice
while rinsing cups. Her father lowers a spoon.

On the terrace, the cat stays in my lap the whole afternoon,
will not let me rise or leave the page,
                              names of things
licked off the pads of her feet.

Down the valley,
Maria Angelita fills her drinking containers
from the fountain in the centre of Almegijár. Her husband
                        waits in shade,
a chair set in stone.

If you listen
        you can hear the years
flipping back through their pages, 1937, 1926,
calendar on the wall of the museum,
Cuban cigars delivered
                by the merchant who rode mule
carrying talcum of rose,
bone hairbrushes, silver from Morocco
                            the dry, white paper
meant for tobacco. Jasmine, oranges,
his load ever lighter.

    The cat cleans herself, relaxes again.
In this heat, I forget
the north, the clamber
    of shoot from ground, its insistence
and speed.

Water runs from mountain to dark stone basins—
hills barren at a distance prove fragrant with herb and vine.
The olive trees' calligraphy
    of black trunk on copper earth,
a precise language, terraced fields
         never finishing a sentence
and heat rising
amidst crickets and cicadas
blurred, from the surface of it all.

Among the misrepresentations,
  here we form the picture of a woman,
some other elegant
character, laughing, unfamiliar as the call of Swainson's thrush,
      as the taste of stone
clear water, as lack of will or voice.
    Slowly, the light
crawls across the valley
and we shift carefully,
remain in shade.

      Sun pierces the haze
and stills everything except the birds,
their casual falling
      through uncharted, unowned space
above the ancient houses.
           I want to pull them from the air.

           Below, the steeple,
leisurely bell and bolero chimneys,
their dark interiors, white washed stone,
        their unrolling
grapevine terraces, dog perched
        on an outcrop of wall,
a once-imagined room,
now a question
      posed without conclusion.

Two

KALEIDOSCOPE, HOW IT DISCLOSES

The spinning wheel of the kaleidoscope
lifts very little into view.

When it ceases, the eye follows movement hidden
in its shapes, begins to read backward.

The interlocking pieces drift
and fuse, the turning

most apparent when it's not,

the mechanism most itself
when it is still.

REGARD

As guests to the party we came with nothing
but our own smouldering bodies, weary

from rusted pulley and rope, their well,
plunging through rock to inner surface

where all things are maintained. The room
made itself over into white shell, and whirled

at its topmost into the black skylight,
an upper portal for candle flame, steam and star.

The women stood with glasses in hand,
took the shining and placed it in air

as praise, grainy, lark-like. Each,
already stepping into careful age, appeared

again, thirty years or more hence.
There was no saving them—

they burned like crystal through the space
where we danced, their heads held high,

floating. They let themselves be regarded
in the ways designed and were not afraid.

IF THERE IS SOMETHING

If there is something, tell me, music.
Music: where in the grass of the delicate?
This light is golden and the wheat so small,
          I don't see how.
My ears tell me no, and when I close my eyes I see
oak trees unfurling the spring and my heart pounds
though I am not climbing the hill. To be away from home.
A car passed this evening, sunk low,
farm family driving the dirt roads, aspen ditches, the dust
rising two days after rain. The husband waved.
I heard a hermit thrush; further and all sound was gone.
Tick of the bush, colt's ears parting the swamp: music,
teenagers in the next quarter section, laughing
before a fuck in the grass. We head into ourselves.
                Where else to go?
I find tobacco tins,
newborn foxes in a culvert. I rub my hands together and
they come, the mother at night far into the fields of her own sharp crooning.
I find the beating organs of a fish. They groan,
they are the words *science* and *wing*, the words *utter terror*. Yes?
But to turn the knot outward, to break it out through the shoulder blades
is like wolf willow, in bloom, in late June, not yet summer, the days
too cold, nothing as it should be, nothing graceful, music
the banging of grasses, wood frogs, tree swallows, the blue flash
of their wing feathers as they draw
                            something through the air.

SUMMER NIGHT

To be back in the field where the deer was.
Somnolent cricket rub, sparking the clear July night.

The wild grass field above the sea, pine rush,
a bell's width of intimacy;
back home,
    lawns shimmered to the lot's edge.

       *

Only years later, we became old.
To be outside, with the insects.
February, and I kill the honeybee that enters, its clotted panic, disintegrating
as the sun falls and cold falls again.
  Night, open-eyed, not watching.

       *

Bluff's insistence, the sea's comb of stone.
Hushed wind; her cloven hoof smoothed the field.
Cricket, gold-skeined
under encircling stars; nothing but to waste the nights of summer.
She grazed around me, for the small wildflowers
  dying in the season's heat,
       her steps erasing the field.
I was one creature huddled in the grass
trying to memorize another. There was no time.

GRADUATES: ST. PETER'S

White candled air,
spring-clear, the boys in tuxes,
girls' braids pulled from their foreheads in long, golden rows.
First warm evening,
sun on the dust of high windows,
      spilling over. The graduates are one quick thought—
they flock, sit down a spell, dropping corsages and coats.

Wind brushes their fingers, scent of willow, anemone,
pale clamendra, recently found—a last field trip to the unbroken
          islands of prairie—native and so common and at home.
Laughing, they think of the big cities.

Please love, be there when they step from the train. A dress hem
catches the light and flames; bursting,
they dance shy sidesteps—
          monks pass like respite from light.

Sweet, sweet, oh so sweet; yellow warbler in the caragana,
sugary amber blossoms someone
told them once to taste and so they did.

SPRING MIGRATION, IN THE FIELD

Orange peel, resin paper, dust, a saffron wave
        pierced the far edge of landscape—
ticks, brome grass, poplar—and unrolled over us;
        we became elsewhere.
It matters I don't know their species;
        I don't want to know.
Rusted wings, a drift of great fires, our shadows before
        they become the dogged
soul at heel. No one covered the silence
        (seed head, leaf); when we stopped
at that compass. River gold, a current of flags—
        shreds of blue sky beyond.
They were the first honest things I have seen.
        Lifting to drift past the trees and
since then I have been dying, or
        I stopped for that
one, dusted moment, our heads lifted,
        thinking how to rise up
how not to coax them down.

NIGHT WALK

Stopped on the track in the field
in front of the hermitage. Breath clouding out,
      lit by my lamp.

Moon falling quarter note into the furrows.
Stars overhead. End of June, chance of a frost.

Lonely, but so kindred it eases
a moment.

Half a mile from the abbey

dew falling and in a little wind
it floats past me,

      maybe mist, snow,
slipping past my face, maybe stars—

and horizontal to the black earth when it comes, and how.

WEB

Small hill, slight spring, season
pulling us through its slow movement,
trackless, still.

Stopped here, caught in the strands of last year's
hexagon: mud, grey grass, twig.
The connections are dusty, they break.
Overrun with what winter has caught,
of what it is capable,
the release notes, the space
before sound, the breathing,
the knot.

SKY AND THE VARIED THRUSH

Slender-ribbed, halting, one by one you lay them down before me.

In the shortened trees around us, your nest, my wishes for this shallow season.

My most secretive bird, grey-brown plumage, smallest of the water-dripping songs.

Lately, silence. I fold things, I pace. And when you come you are mute and I dislike you.

Can you explain this awakening to the carved-out hills?

Where am I?—you would know. Below us, these ridges of dust and green,

a world remaking itself, a dozen needles at a time.

Brown plumage, delicate wordlessness, most beautiful of all.

MEASURE

Grace note, come in, come in! All around the cabin: sky,
through the windows,
                in the grass, the animals: sky.
And because we cannot live in lyric
the bitter-sweet taste of notation
strings against the ear. The bragging fireweed along the hill's edge,
the heavy tongue of the fawn.

Sharp night, silver fish of northern lights.
Gulls in the day from the lake, mussed feathers,
quick glide of summer's spread across the pines.
        They are black here, and cold—quick!

But it's not fine,
it's vestige of winter, held stubborn
through two months of trick days, everything
bloom and die, bloom and die.

Shut rock, lichen, crisp wind, faster dusk.
                      Fine, then.
In the branches of the pines I see
a dry fist of pleasure in long days;
see it ball itself smaller, strike the edge of the ridge until rocks
cling and tumble, home again, thinking home, again,
        again.

    I am the rest, between measures,
       where the stream twists
amid sandstone and moss, wanting down, wanting low.
The end note nowhere loving or constant:
       a fracas; a leap of every animal
off the cliff to a place the wind can't go.

WINTER: ARIA DA CAPO

I.

Clarity: Glenn Gould fingers over the snow:
a landscape that melts as we imagine it real.
The afternoon scene, another melancholic knowledge—
    step into it, grow!

    The drains clatter.
Understanding no more, we nod at the system
of notes, methodical, placed,
tracks of one hand spreading to chord.

Shafts of bracken and black earth open
    between keys.

II.

Refrain. His sleeve grazes the wood's grained heart.

It is not clean or free, and in the 1954 recording
with weighted piano, its underwater resonance
is raw, a muffled pendulum's banter.

Rest. Then
the small waterfall,
twice, his fingers following one another over the snow.
There, and

there, it goes on forever,
        perfect, useless,
from bright to dark and behind him
no trace of where he's been.

LIES IN THE FIELD LIKE THE SKY

Just before the Anerley valley in Saskatchewan,
where dust feeds a hollow that once was a town,

he stops the car and parks for the night, sleeps
in one of the wheat fields his mother left him when she died.

A late August night cools his body as he waits out the dark
half a mile above the train tracks, small house and wild horses

part of him could consider home. The sky, as he watches
its circling stars, reminds him of the sky over the village of Kagbeni

in the Kali Gandaki valley, the girl there who slept
in her shoes, holding her two younger sisters.

She worked in the kitchen behind swirling steam,
boiling tea in pots with milk and sugar until all collided

into a sweetness that mingled with the dung fire
in the stove and her body, her red cheeks,

the dry riverbed on the backs of her hands.
The river that shaped the valley carved through her life,

took more every year, though horses grazed
along its edges through the night and it was tamed

into clear pathways leading to the fields. With her
he walked along the cut channels, stones in his pocket,

stones forming his heart's cage, the girl beside him; kissed her
until she lay down in the field, her eyes on the stars.

He remembers it this way, though it may have been he only
braided her hair, touching in passing the nape of her neck,

its warmth twisting against him the way the river of air
in Saskatchewan flows over him the night before he descends

to what's left of his family, the aunt with animals,
a prospering farm, a cancerous husband

who waited in newly contemplative silence for the lift
of an organ from his body; a home by the remains of a station

the train no longer slows for. He returns to help
the aunt with whatever she needs him for;

the daily chores of hay and feed for llamas, sheep and cows,
cleaning, mending, or simply matching her dip for dip

from the bottomless bottle of scotch which will occupy a shelf
above the table, but never returns there for long.

The returning is the most difficult, knowing that last time
he walked from valley up coulee to prairie he found,

by the small granite block which signifies the place,
something which might have been bone from his mother's remains;

from hip, or shoulder, a place to hold
imaginary wings drawn by a child one evening years ago,

bursting from the sides of a girl, a muscled
horse, field and sky crayon bright behind.

His mother's family kept horses in the valley,
but they have been wild now for two generations

running from him as he rose through the ravine, bolting
in the sun from one grass river to another,

their manes tangled with vetch and ladies tresses.
His heart beat fast then, startled to see

their dark heads nodding, as it beat
when he was with the girl in Nepal, felt her skin against his.

Day and night, the sound of bells echoed up and down
that larger valley, yak and mule trains carrying salt, kerosene,

rice and plastic up the trail from one country
to another, bells strung on a cord that wore away pelt

until the hide shone black with callus and dry blood.
She would watch them from the doorway of the kitchen,

negotiating the small paths of the village,
the stone buildings intimate.

If he was not walking in the hills, he would stand beside her,
her eyes following the train, each bell's ringing

vibrating the flagstones, a space already too small,
their arms brushing, breath falling together.

She lived at ten thousand feet, and never followed
the valley lower; he fell into her breath's rhythm the way, lying

at the edge of Anerley a year later, he knows he will fall
back into his aunt's life and they will both feel

one taking care of the other. When he walks each evening
she does not come with him. The ties

are covered with dust and seed and printed
with the unshod hooves of horses, coulees curling on each side,

prairie fed into valley in an endless current. Her figure recedes,
waiting with the dogs on the road, and when he turns to look

she is woman, then stick, then crow, then point.
He lies in the field through the night, car beside him.

The crickets trill, stars perambulate, valley falls into itself,
dust more than water shaping it. He thinks again of the girl

whose nape he knows from memory as completely
as the valley he lies above, the train of mules lurching

away, steam hanging in the air. The hearts of the animals
bang against their chests, eyes on the next descent.

Three

THEORY

When I imagine a field
I see the field above me. A bowl of green,
base at the crown of the head, unfurling, a tug up and out.
When I imagine again,
a wishbone splits in two, like frog song, like grasses
in my summer's selfish drought; a sliding scale (a dry soul).
In design, a key signature: *A* is the balanced page,
harmonized, Bach's *Aria da Capo*, steady rain, Fibonacci's shell
spiralling over the grain.

Ethics is not beautiful,
but the green bowl rising,
and falling
open,
away from itself.

STARS; CHILDHOOD

Consider the first moment
we were told stars
still shone in the day,
their light lost in blue.

Everything in that
instant.
Trees twisting, in bursts,
to leaf; the milk surface of the pond,

birds and shadows
on the spattering ground, the rain—
each combustion of *goodbye*,
goodbye.

STATION

We keep the things that heal and hurt us most.
From an old lover, a poem once my favourite

sung every note at once. My father's brief letter,
carried as talisman against danger for years

on the dash. Still, I hit the deer.
Other things, the asbestos that killed your father,

a sample snug in a drawer in your sister's cottage, a lyric:
gifted, durable, calm; a caterpillar losing its skin

for another; burrowed in a lung,
quietly breathing. Tonight, we conceive no one.

We make love and the pain of losing
shines across my skin—such pleasure this losing.

The vial was tightly stopped but it took
only one false step in the mine to halt things,

to loose the top. Brought back at fourteen by village police
for smashing yet another window, what could you say

of grieving? That it is contained
in a small glass vial. That it is easily mixed

with paper clips, toothpicks, pencils, the charm
from a Christmas cracker. Your parents,

a photo of their 1957 wedding car ride,
her absolute resolve, his luck.

I don't know when or if our child will appear.
These would be stories.

Don't you dare loose the stopper, I will cry
to anyone who tries. We should leave the things

that harm us in the ground.
You leapt across country, time zone, climate—

we found one another. But I do not throw the letter away,
nor the poem. They slide in drawers when we reach,

and the mine is just down the road.
Someday my father will die; the place

will be the one I return to the rest of my life,
to recall the sorrow, to swim past dark in its dry husk.

LETTER TO LUKE, WHO IS HERE WITH ME IN BUBIÓN

Our rented house is surrounded by garden.
Close by, a river, and all around
the village, taps from which we drink.
Outside the window,
avocado tree, potato patch, night-blooming jasmine,
three climbing roses and a grape vine;
you sense them coming through the window in little thrills.
The steeple is west, along the sun's path before it falls
behind the mountain. Paintbrush, cypress,
white-washed stone of the neighbour's house,
his dog calm, his child gathering water,
her hair loose and feet bare
at eleven at night.
She carries it perfectly
and does not spill a drop.

To the south we can see one hundred miles,
the hills verdant with herbs.

Love, I cannot stop anything anymore and
it may all be different next time—
cricket, mole or rat claim
more than the corners of these stone rooms.

As we move,
the losses inside us keep pace, dependable
as darkness at this latitude—
there will always be less
of the one we want.

RETURN OF THE NUTHATCHES

Oh so that's how it is. Flocks,
or nothing.
The sky breaks open, out comes summer,
kept until now in the glassy pond,
the water bugs black, glossy shells, the wind.

Push it to the other side.
The current out of a forest is a knot of birds
        that swells upside down in the branches.
Almost too late, just in time,
tempo, temper, flutter of their cheep, crack and plummet. Rise.
Something in the mid-level now, right where
the trees become preposterous, divine.

Or continuation.
They spill from the branches, foiling grubs
and predictions against all odds;
the pond expands

    into fall; warm night wind in the city,
    rain on its surface,
    but the roads don't deepen
    with ruts and repetitions
    as storms swell streams, cut-banks and gutters.

To search the ground for seeds,
concrete for the right hue. Here is the heart at one stage,
then another; here is the heart at another.

CONSIDERING MY FATHER

He dips his oars into the bay. Ripples trail beside the tender
as he circles to the next stroke. Late summer, late night,

and phosphorescence charts his path through the dark,
a spread of pasture and shallows, anchored hull.

He knows it better than he knows his daughters, four
fingers pulling an oar. The sweep and plunge of their eyes,

the farthest among them, her hands in long grasses
like a tangle of kelp, the field like water, soil sand

at the sea's edge. She comes in from the garden,
fills a glass, waters the plants on the sill. The water

runs along the edge like water on the length of an oar.
He will not stop. The bay a hollow he anchors in,

green mirror and endless blur. A field at the head is isthmus
of wild grass, sand, clover. He has never been there,

never landed. Past the small spit of pasture, rock,
a barge dragged to shore, the other side—water, again.

THIS PERFORMANCE OF ROWING
THROUGH THE DARK AND STARS

Notes like pencilled lines when they first begin, then shapes
and the shapes concentrate, become more,

and they are birds, and bells, and tongues, and they congregate.
There are acres of silence like bays or fields between them.

The bay with phosphorescence in summer. July,
August. Time to row through darkness, enclosed,

a shell of stars, without worry, wonder
or urgency for his love. Striking the bell at the bay's head,

flight of sound over water. Here are the horns.
There is a heart; his, mine, unwinding,

counted hours on a watch; before the music began
we turned them off together. A world bounded by walking

distances from a boat. Pasture of cowslip, salt; trail to the house
that sold pies, coffee; road to the ferry dock with red railings.

Low tide hollows the clams sat in. Deep set, waiting
in sand. Rake striking shell, the teeth-on-edge sound

of grains against the tines. Everything
with its tether attached: anchor line, bow line, painter,

mooring, their concentric circles drawn
in invisible ink—no ripple to say we were there. Underwater,

rocks disturbed, and a midden of shells, swinging down,
ringing against the heaviness of saltwater,

each long since fallen from its pair.

AS WATER IS TO INLANDS

-for my father

We circled the islands and it was our knot. Bowline,
two half hitches, hold it fast. To know

what you knew of charted shorelines, wing-on-wing,
rounding an architecture of sandstone, dragging the well

of tide pool. Intricate inlet, passage,
hidden shoal and flashing mark. Music in the hold,

food in the keel's damp recess and dark, these
simple stores and lockers, all in accordance with current.

If I remove myself to be always interior, to see dry vines
colour a courtyard, know their brilliance not as my own,

does this resolve somnolent hours, sculling
without sound as seal or otter attended,

the hump of the dinghy's bow a breath held
against the bay? To hear Clementi's Concerto in D is to desire water.

You would not take us inland, I knew nothing of roads—
a car's stern will not swing out when its course is changed—

cried when we cycled the flattest island.
The sheer energy required to move such a small body.

Wind on the sea made light break into a thousand spells
you cast again with jib and pole. Qualicum, Southerly,

Saanich; a Squamish williwaw falls
down coast range to strait. Pour down the dust-dark

necks of mountains to their well centre, water
sparse and clear, its depths unsounded.

WHEN ALL IS SAID OR DONE

I prefer the orchestra's moment of tuning
to the performance. Then, unscored octaves,

thirds and melodic fourths fill us with the music
a forest of birds makes without meaning. Oboes

lead violins into synchrony, wind instruments
back to the birds they once were. Then my father

sits again beside me, moving pen and papers
from one breast pocket to the other. Falling

to sleep near the end of the second movement,
I will have heart, rib and generous muscle

to lean on, the same presence musicians find
before playing and plunge toward, a perfection

of notes caught on the page. Give me that moment,
or the other, when my father's movement wakes me,

and I lift from his chest to the waterfall
of applause around us. The orchestra joins, stands,

the conductor disappears offstage.
They are exhausted, emptied of what they strained toward,

and, because no longer straining, whole.
I want nothing more. Bring my father back to me

in octaves, in the cacophony of tune and scale, the music
of intelligent hands coming together in praise.

THE REFLECTING POOL

Illuminated by early evening sun, we walked to where the pool lies,
into the yielding forest, which shrugged when we tried to praise.

Inside its amalgam of shadow and cessation, the glassy pond
aimed its whole self down to the centre of the earth.

There was another world inside. Taut against the stick
and moss disorder, the water inscribed edge without movement.

It loved so thoroughly the small branches of the overhanging fir,
the dead, spindled tumbles of emptied pine cones, the luminescence

of twinflower, wolf moss, fairy cup, mud. Its reaching became
an imitating eye, and the mirror elegy to what it loved.

Because it chose, we could see all things twice, and so had the chance
of glimpsing, the second time, what we always first ignore.

And as the water fell away, it took the image of the forest
and stretched it to the greenest shadows, taking our eyes

further and further down, and in. Its lofted breadth
ravelled the tapestry, learned every movement, armed gravity,

arraying knowledge in its rightness and its pull.

Four

LATE AUGUST: YIELDING

Its beginning is train song,
late at night, in the distance,
and the roar of the wheels
as they pass in the dark.

It could be wind, more
than metal on metal
thundering a corridor
through the valley.

Three times
the whistle blows, long,
longer, then
pure sorrow.

RIVER, BUT NO EDGE

Robin's three call perpetua springs out
two streets from the sea, and still, the clamour,
the clang and pearl of thought.
Bells sound from the strait, brass plums
cradling dark, enclosed by fog, breath,
an hour of breathing at three AM, awake; it comes in surges,
it finds the thing, it grasps, it holds.

THE REFLECTING POOL, MOUNT HELMCKEN: AFTERWORD

And the beat
of my bulldozer heart.
This forest of rivened hope.
This cartilage of pine
and spindled fir, the *water pipes,*
the *blacktop* carve of road.

Manzanita—
      daughter of arbutus and salal,
little apple, wreathed,
rusted entrance to the forest pool—

The peak; *cleared brush*. The yielding forest,
which shrugged,
      and the reflection
which returns to the deep green point of reference.
Muscle catches, splays forward
while the pool blinks—freezes,
cleaves from its assessed value.
    The pond and its bright eye *can go.*
And so it goes. And so it goes.

Summer's Variations

WORK

Vine flowering honeysuckle, only the junco sings.
A woman in the morning, her talkative guests,
the continuous haze of sky. She quits
the perfect job before breakfast, steps out into the day,
drains clattering.

Not just the perspective, not the cleanliness.
Though that, too, is a surprising reward.
What she is thinking can be played with extended pedal,
in chord, on an old, bird piano. Rising,
like the molecules of summer air in cohesion,
not collision, into mares' tails of stratus, layered,
more complicated than the brute singularity of the battleship nimbus.
The world turns away.

Or, she turns away from the world.
Alexandria, or its nearest approximation,
hovers ahead on the road.
The mirage of her clearest dream is not a mirage,
it is a breathlessness, it does not know, and the transmission
may be stalled, or it may grind through the morning
toward afternoon's repose. The cured grass
empty of colour, sanctifying, terrible.
How beautiful, the empty hand that has let it all go,

chaff loosening, pollen creeping, the cones of the pine
unclenching their children fists one scale at a time,
all at once in the heat, one at, all at a time.

TRILL

To neglect the imagination. Just as dangerous a path
as the incessant beauty you craved as a child.
Weil to know the inner limits;
to know the outer, an unnamable bird in the willow,
      its rising-falling trill.

Keep the idea: she lands on you, and together you sleep
the afternoon heat and wind back into night.
                      She can land, she well may.

Her other, possible names: winter wren, chipping sparrow,
calliope's hummingbird—song may come
not from the throat but the wing.
Out in the strait, church peal of the current bell,
marking not highest or lowest but fastest flow—
                      the midpoint of flight,
the centre of thought—mind's smooth river
rushing through other, stationary water. The cliffs

of its sinkholes, smoothness of its sheer walls
and perch shadows of expansion, plunge and pull.

      Porlier Pass: water travels out during flood, not in.
Calliope's hummingbird arcs into a territorial, ferocious climb,
                          sears through the peak,

       begins to dive.
The air tunes her feathers to the key
of small forest stream played *fuerte*
in an echo chamber; let loose it is all insensate,

it refuses as it sings.

STILLNESS

The stillness in every season is extreme for a moment,
then soon, gone,
replaced, indistinctly, by continuation.
        When the cicadas begin,
the junco is a fugitive rustle in the leaves, now moving,
now waiting.
We find things altering; a mirage of warmth or cold
marks the midpoint, a small centre of spinning, a slow freeze—
like the sea scene in *The Four Hundred Blows*, when Antoine arrives
at the expanse of the wave
        and is drawn in.
Now then, I said, I go to meet that which I liken to.
                                Always, the entry
and then the dreaming in.   Then.
We do not remember exactly what follows:
dailiness goes on unmarked
as the edges of a doorway or a mirror.
It is the centre that interests, so this we recall.
The cicadas stop, begin again, then end.

I wish I could promise a concern
that would remain. That I might promise an attention
which gave its word not to wander, not to lull. There,
the rustle of the wing, the molted feathers dislodging,

the flight across the terrace; there,
the song stitching the portal through which all of it comes;
there, the entry, watery, dark, flowing,
and we are in and it has flown.

SILENCE

In *Vivre sa vie*, Parain tells Nana
there is a small death which must occur in the self
before it can surface to its second life;
out of silence—a pass through darkness—we emerge.

And so, in the centre of Paris, during its longest days,
she is living through a death within herself.
Planned, executed
in collusion with many forces, its outcome unknown.
Outside, the regular, bunch-leafed trees
line Champs Elysees. Their structured waving,
their safe harbours. She sits in the booth, smoking;
she looks like any other woman.

The philosopher leans back in his seat
and his face is a photograph. The trees race
into the distance until a building prevents
their going any further, and unexpectedly,
they veer off the screen.
We do not see them again.

RUMMAGE

One by one the valves open, seal shut behind.
Trapped: white poplar; dust from the streets
of Mérida; the words *green up* and the word *quiero*;
a dry pine with peeling bark recalling the arbutus, its sister,
the green skin shining deep in the ruddy limbs;
hermit thrushes, by the hundreds,
song that keeps moving;
an oarlock with yellow varnished oar—
its mate wanting the other—lost?
Three deer that look up, meet my gaze—one at Notikewin,
one in the field above the sea, the third, my
circling companion, reason to swim summer's night,
reason grief takes so long to find, so long to take leave.
A blue, hooded coat; limpets; a piece of unforged silver;
my father's foot scribing the air, conductor of the evening's
thunderstorm; rain on the sea, pushed before the storm;
rain on the sea as the canoe rounded Coal Island shallows
last spring, shell shallows, oyster and sea star; full—
no, it's empty, the poplars are stretching through my throat,
empty—no, it's full, and there will be, there must be
more.

NOTES & ACKNOWLEDGEMENTS

Some of these poems first appeared in the following journals and magazines: *The Antigonish Review, Arc, CV2, Descant, Event, The Fiddlehead, Prism International* and *The Wascana Review*. "The Reflecting Pool" also appeared in *The Best of Canadian Poetry in English, 2008,* ed. Stephanie Bolster, Tightrope Books 2008. Thanks to the editors of these publications.

"Regard" was first published in High Ground Press's "Companions" Broadsheet Series, 2005, and was written as companion for "Things of August," by Wallace Stevens.

The title "Lies in the Field like the Sky" is taken from Michael Ondaatje's *Coming Through Slaughter*.

The italicized line in "Stillness" is taken from Jorie Graham's *Region of Unlikeness*. "Stillness" owes much to Elizabeth Bishop's "At the Fishhouses," as well as to Truffaut.

My thanks for keen editorial attendance and care to Beth Follett of Pedlar.

"Spring Migration" is for Tim Lilburn, Don McKay, Jan Zwicky and *In the Field* participants. As well, my gratitude for the June conversations which took place at St. Peter's College, to the monks of the Abbey, and especially to Don, for months of longhand letter exploration through the territories of silence.

"Sky and the Varied Thrush" and "Measure" are for the wild around Notikewin, Clear Hills and Torrens Fire Lookouts, Alberta, where I spent five northern summers. What little I know of how to listen was relearned there.

Thanks to the BC Arts Council, the Canada Council for the Arts and The Banff Centre; and Fonda Nacional para la Cultura y las Artes (FONCA), Mexico, for time, space and support, during which much of this book was completed.

To Kris Elder, Emilia Nielsen, Wanda Power, Bren Simmers, Anna Swanson and all the lovelies, chosen family. To those of Mérida and Banff, Eduardo Milán's "No hay porqué, hay órdenes de canto." Thanks to Bill Stenson for starting it all, and to Derk Wynand—wholeheartedly amazing teachers.

To my whole, unruly family, but especially to my mother, for teaching me gardens, and my father, for playing harmonica in the rain on Star Bright.

To Luke Carson, first and last reader, for letting me know, in his beautiful way, when things were beginning to come together.

BREN SIMMERS

MALEEA ACKER lives on Vancouver Island. Her work has been published in journals such as *The Fiddlehead*, *The Malahat Review*, *Prism International*, *Descant*, *Event*, and the anthologies *Best Canadian Poetry in English, 2008* and *Rocksalt*. She has an MFA from the University of Victoria and teaches Writing at Camosun College.